THE THIRTY-SIXTH DIVISION

IN

THE GREAT WAR

" ... WE, DEPARTING, LEAVE BEHIND US.
FOOT-PRINTS ON THE SANDS OF TIME."

Published in France by

THE ARROWHEAD,

DIVISIONAL NEWSPAPER

A. E. F.

TO THE MEMORY

OF OUR FALLEN COMRADES,

WHO PAID THE PRICE FOR THE PEACE

WE NOW ENJOY,

THIS BOOK IS REVERENTLY

DELICATED.

Major General William R. Smith.

SUMMARY 0F ACTIVITES OF THE

36th DIVISION

The 36th Division was organized during August and September of 1917, from National Guard organizations of Texas and Oklahoma, The old National Guard. recruited to war strength, was used as a nucleus for the Division, and 8,500 drafted men were assigned to the Division at various times.

The Division was trained at Camp Bowie, Fort Worth, Texas, until July 1918, when the overseas movement began. During this training period the Division was under the command of Major General E. St. John Greble, who was reduced because of physical disability to the rank of Brigadier General, and was succeeded upon the commencement of overseas movement by Major General William R. Smith. The 36th Division was composed of the following units: 71st Infantry Brigade under command of Brigadier General Henry Hutchings, formely Adjutant General, State of Texas. 72nd Infantry Brigade under command of Brigadier General John A. Hulen, also an officer of the Texas National Guard. General Hutchins was succeeded by Brigadier General Pegram Whitworth, shortly after the Division arrived overseas. Brigadier General George Blakeley, of the Coast Artillery was in command of the 61st Field Artillery Brigade.

The overseas movement was begun July 5th, 1918, and completed about August 15th.

The 36th Division consists of the following organizations :

36th Division Headquarters

36th Division Headquarters Troop

36th Military Police Company

111th Field Signal Battalion

131st Machine Gun Battali n

71st Infantry Brigade : —

    141st Infantry

    142nd Infantry

    132nd Machine Gun Battalion

71 Infantry Brigade : —

    143rd Infantry

    144th Infantry

    133rd Machine Gun Battalion

61st Field Artillery Brigade : —

    131st Field Artillery — 3 inch Guns

    132nd Field Artillery — 3 inch Guns

    133rd Field Artillery — 6 inch Guns

    111th Trench Mortar Battery

    111th Ammunition Train

111th Engineers and Engineer Train

111th Sanitary Train

    Ambulance Companies 141, 142, 143, 144,

    Field Hospitals 141, 142, 143, 144.

111th Supply Train

Major General William R. Smith assumed command of the Division at the Port of Embarkation. On arrival in France the Infantry sections of the Division were sent to the Bar-sur-Aube (13th) Training Area, where they remained untill September 26th.

The Artillery Brigade trained at Coetquidan, but never rejoined the Division after their arrival in France, and, though the Division had its fling at the front, the 61st Artillery never saw action.

On September 11th, 1918, the 111th Engineers were detatched from the Division and assigned to the American First Army as Corps Engineers of the 1st A. C., with which organization they remained untill after the signing of the Armistice. They participated in the St-Mihiel Drive and operated throughout the Meuse-Argonne Offensive.

The Division, minus the Engineers and Artillery Brigade, left the Bar-sur-Aube Area September 26th, 1918, moving to the Pocancy Area as part of the Armies Reserve of the French Group of Armies of the center — General Meistre. On October 3rd, 1918, the Division was transfered to the Fourth French Army under General Gouraud. It was with this French Army that the Division fought in the Champagne, and thereby won its right to a place in the history of the Combat Units of the A. E. E.

SUMMARY OF ACTIVITIES AT THE FRONT

Oct. 4th. — The 71st Brigade moved to the Suippes-Somme-Suippes-Area.

Octr 5th. — The 71st Brigade was transfered to the 21st Corps French Army, with the Second Division, Américan. During the night of the 6th the Brigade relieved the front line of the Second Division southeast of St-Etienne, the remainder of the Division begining its movement to the Suippes-Somme-Suippes Area,

Oct. 8th — The 71st Brigade, with the 141st Inf. on the right and the 142nd Inf. on the left, launched its first attack between St. Etienne-a Arnes and Medeah Farm, capturing approximately 600 prisoners and breaking the backbone of the German resistence north of Blanc Mont.

Oct. 10th. — The 36th Division established its Post of Command in old German dug-outs in Somme-Py, completing the relief of the Second Division, except for the Artillery, Engineers, and certain supply elements. In all its operation the 36th Division was ably supported by the 12th, 15th, and 17th Art. Regiments of the Second Division.

Oct. 10-11 — The Boche was given no pause for breath. Th 72nd Brigade, passing through the 71st, took up the fight and advanced to the Aisne River, hard on the heels of the retreating Germans.

Oct. 12-27 — The Division took up a line of resistence on th hills just south of the Aisne River, and remained here untill the 27th, making preparations for the crossing of the river and Ardennes Canal.

Oct. 27th. — The 71st Brigade, after shifting its front slightly carried out a brilliant local operation at Forest Farm, bringing in 194 prisoners of the Prussian Guard. Four Officers were included in the haul. The American casualties totaled fifty ;-fourteen killed and thirty-six wounded.

Oct. 27-28 — After twenty one days of fighting the Division was relieved by the 22nd French Division. Moving from the front the Division reached the Conde-en-Barrois Area on Nov. 3rd, as a part of the Armies Reserve of the First American Army.

Nov. 4th-18th — During these days the Division remained in the Conde-en-Barrsis area, taking in replacements and re-equipping for the future fighting on another front. At the time of the signing of the Armistice it was the intention of the high Command to use the 36th on the left flank of the Second American Army in the drive toward Metz.

Nov. 18-22 — The Division at this time was on the march from the Conde-en-Barrois area to the 16th Trainin Area, Tonnerre, Yonne.

SUM TOTALS.

Total advance of the Division — 21 kilometers (13 1/8 miles)

Totol prisoners captured by troops of this Division — 813

Total materiel captured ; — 3 pieces heavy artillery ; 6 pieces light artillery ; - 17 trench mortars ; - 277 machinus guns.

Value of Munitions and Materiel captured in Dumps, etc ; - 10.000.000.00 - Ten million dollars.

THE PRICE THEY PAID

Total Casualties ; - Killed in action, - 21 officers ; 469 men.
Died of Wounds ; - 4 officers ; 70 men.
Gassed ; - 17 officers ; - 329 men.
Slightly Wounded ; - 42 officers ; 896 men.
Wounded, Severely ; - 39 officers ; 474 men.
Wounded, degree undetermined ; - 5 officers ; - 141 men.
Missing ; - 94
Total Casuatlies ; - 2.601 officers and men.

FOR VALOR

Number of D. S. C. s awarded ; - 30
Number of Croix de Guerres ; - 129
Congressionnal Medals of Honor ; - 2

GENERAL ORDER, HEADQUARTERS;
21st A.C. (French) Oct. 14th, 1918

The 36th Division, U.S., recently organized, and still not fully equipped, received during the night of the 6th-7th October, the order to relieve, under conditions particularly delicate, the Second Division, to drive out the enemy fron the heights to the North of St. Etienne-a Arnes and to push him back to the Aisne.

Althougt being under fire for the first time, the young soldiers of Gen. Smith rivaling in push and tenacity, with the older and valient regiments of Gen. Lejune, accomplished their mission fully. All can be proud of the work done. To all, the General commanding the Army Corps, is happy to express his cordial appreciation, gratitude and best wishes for future successes. The past is an assurance of the future.

GENERAL NAULIN,

Commanding Army Corps."

A TELEPHONE MESSAGE FROM CORPS,

Oct. 16th.

The General commanding the Corps wishes to congratulate the General commanding the 36th Division and the members of his command, upon the prompt compliance with Corps orders in the capturing of German prisoners on the night of October 14th."

1. Maj.-Gen. Wm. R. Smith.

1. Maj.Gen. Wm. R. Smith - 2. Brig.-Gen. Pegram Whitworth.

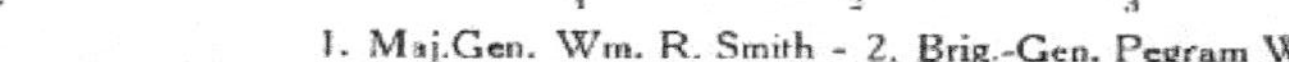

The Division Staff

The Suippes — Somme-Py road through the Hindenberg line

Souain, showing, effect of four years bombardment.

Gouraud's-prepared Line of Defense North of Suippes, passed through by 36 th Division troops enroute to the front.

German water station south of Mont Blanc. Principal source of supply for 36 th Division troops during the St-Etienne fight Oct. 6 to 12.

P. C. 141 st Infantry Oct. 7 to Oct. 12.

P. C. 142 nd Infantry during St-Etienne fight Oct. 6 to 12.

P. C. 2 nd Batallion 142 nd Infantry Oct. 8 th.

Dugout in St-Etienne used as P.C. by 3rd batt. 142nd Inf. Oct. 9th by 2nd batt. 142nd Inf. Oct. 10th and by Reg. command. Oct. 11th.

Stretch of woods a Km. soûth of St-Etienne. This shows effects of artillery fire.

Church at St-Etienne used by German snipers Oct. 8.

Medeah Ferme. A principal landmark in the operations North of Somme-Py.

German Pill Box at eastern edge of St-Etienne.

The P. C. C. at Somme-Py Oct. 10-12

A German gun captured by the 36th Division North of St. Etienne Oct. 11th.

German Engineer dump at St. Etienne Captured by the 36th. Division Oct. 11th.

C..... O.R...... the ... d of Beacon's Hill

P. C. of 72 nd Brigade Oct. 10 th.

Section of Somme-Py — St-Etienne road over Mont-Blanc showing Germain camouflage.

Graves of 137 officers and enlisted men of 36th Division killed during
the St-Etienne fight Oct. 8-11.

Moscou Fme building used as P. C. by various batallions of the 72 nd Brigade.

P. C. of 36 th Division at Dricourt Oct. 12 th to Oct. 28 th.

Barton's Hill from St. Etienne cemetery.

View of the nills south of the Aisne on which the line of resistance of the
36th Division was fixed Oct. 15 to Oct. 28th,

Enemy munition dump S.E. of Mont St-Remy captured by 73rd Division (French) and 36th Division (American). Oct. 12th.

Beaumont Fme.

Ruins of Attigny

Brick yard east of Attigny prominent in the operations of the 36 th Division Oct. 12 to Oct. 28 th.

Ruins of Givry.

Forest Fme.

German artillery emplacement just N. E. of St. Etienne.

Boche wire, Forest Fme. Operation. (Voncq in distance).

Bridge over the Ardennes canal destroyed during retreat by the enemy, probably Oct. 27th during Forest Fine. Operation.

German strong point at N. W. end of forest Fme, showing wanton and needless destruction of apple orchards, by the enemy.

IMPRIMERIE
LÉON DAUER
29, rue du Terrage
PARIS (X')
Téléph. Nord 34-40